The Plan That Never *Fails*

JESUS IS LORD

KENNETH
COPELAND
PUBLICATIONS

Unless otherwise noted, all scripture is from the *King James Version* of the Bible.

The Plan That Never Fails

ISBN 978-1-60463-092-3 30-0069

15 14 13 12 11 10 6 5 4 3 2 1

Kenneth Copeland Publications
Fort Worth, TX 76192-0001

For more information about Kenneth Copeland Ministries, call 800-600-7395 or visit www.kcm.org.

The Plan That Never *Fails*

Have you noticed how many people are coming up with plans for us these days? Politicians, media pundits, financial advisors—they all seem to have a plan for our future and our economic security.

I've never heard so many plans as I have in recent times. They have plans to get rid of our clunker cars. Plans to help us buy houses. Plans to fund our retirement. Plans for our health care.

To put it as politely as I can, I've never heard so much bull.

Of course, that's not what the planners call it. They think their ideas are brilliant. But they're wrong. Because their ideas don't include God, they fall into the scriptural category of the "way which seemeth right unto a man, but the end thereof are the ways of death" (Proverbs 14:12).

That's why the Lord warned me about them in advance. In October 2008, He spoke to me one morning in my study in a powerful way and said:

Don't pay attention to or make any plans based on what the media say or what the politicians are saying. Pay attention to Me.... All the other voices will have a plan, a word, an idea, for your future and security. Don't listen to Babylon's system. It has fallen apart. My system is stronger than ever. My kingdom is flourishing and THE BLESSING is the place to be. Keep your eyes on My Word. Listen to it. It will guide you. I will perform it. Love Me. Love My people as I have loved you.... Love never fails and neither does My plan. Be very cautious to stay completely clean from covetousness. First Timothy 6:10 must live in the forefront of your thinking. If you will do these things and continue therein, you will come into your wealthy place.

Covetousness Is Crippling

When the Lord said that to me, I began studying and praying especially over the part about covetousness. I had always assumed it just meant *coveting*, "wanting to take for yourself something that belongs to someone else." I equated it with the command in Exodus 20:17 which says, "Thou shalt not covet thy neighbour's house, thou shalt not covet thy neighbour's wife... nor any thing that is thy neighbour's."

But actually, coveting and covetousness are two different things. Covetousness is a way of thinking that eventually leads to coveting. It's a natural, carnal mindset that doesn't include God.

Most of us were trained in it by our parents' generation. We were raised to believe as the world does—that we are responsible for meeting our own material needs and wants. We were brought up to think we have to go out and gather up money for ourselves—that we have to make our own living.

We grew up hearing Mom and Dad and Grandma say things like, "Now listen to me, child. You better make good grades in school because if you don't, you won't get into college, and if you don't go to college, you'll never be able to get a good job. You'll be poor your whole life."

It never occurs to most Christians that there's anything wrong with that perspective. They don't realize it's based on the logic of the world and doesn't include an ounce of faith in God. They just accept it, and make their financial decisions accordingly.

Instead of asking, "What does God want me to do? What does He have planned for me?" they ask, "How can I make enough money to meet my needs?" Then they come up with a way that seems right to them but ends up in death.

That kind of *thinking*—not the world's economy—is what is crippling believers financially these days. It's a covetous mindset and it is cutting them off from THE BLESSING of God. Even worse, it's a deadly way of thinking that eventually leads to financial manipulation, cheating, theft and all other kinds of evil.

"Wait a minute, Brother Copeland," you might say, "I thought the love of money is the root of all evil."

It is. But covetous thinking is what turns people into money-lovers. First Timothy 6:9-10 says it this way: "They that will be rich fall into temptation and a snare, and into many foolish and hurtful lusts, which drown men in destruction and perdition. For the love of money is the root of all evil: which while some coveted after, they have erred from the faith, and pierced themselves through with many sorrows."

Notice that passage refers to "they that will be rich." It's not talking about people who trust THE BLESSING of the Lord to make them rich and add no sorrow with it (Proverbs 10:22). It's talking about people who are trying to get rich by their own willpower and human ingenuity. It's talking about "the ungodly, who prosper in the world" (Psalm 73:12) by gathering up finances for themselves, and God isn't any part of it.

That's covetousness, and it leads to the love of money and all kinds of sorrowful, evil things. It leads people to make decisions that seem right but turn out to be deadly.

Right Question/Wrong Answer

There's a story in Luke 12 that reveals how truly dangerous covetousness is. Jesus told it in response to a man who called out to Him right in the middle of a teaching meeting and said, "Master, speak to my brother, that he divide the inheritance with me" (verse 13). I suppose the guy was expecting Jesus to issue a financial judgment right then and there. But instead He gave him (and all the rest of us) an earful about the underlying issue. He said: "Take heed, and beware of covetousness: for a man's life consisteth not in the abundance of the things which he possesseth" (verse 15).

The phrase *take heed* means "wake up; look and listen; beware or be very cautious." It describes a state of mind referred to in aviation as *situational awareness.* To a pilot, situational awareness means he knows what's going on around him every minute of the flight, so if something malfunctions, he detects it and deals with it before it wrecks the airplane. That's the way we must be where covetousness is concerned. We must always be aware and on guard against it.

Jesus drove home that point by telling about a man—not a fictional character but a real person—who lost his situational awareness and let covetousness wreck his life.

> The ground of a certain rich man brought forth plentifully: And he thought within himself, saying, What shall I do, because I have no room where to bestow

> my fruits? And he said, This will I do: I will pull down my barns, and build greater; and there will I bestow all my fruits and my goods. And I will say to my soul, Soul, thou hast much goods laid up for many years; take thine ease, eat, drink, and be merry (verses 16-19).

Notice the initial question the rich man asked was a good one. I believe God actually inspired it. He put it in the rich man's spirit to get his attention because the man had been focusing completely on himself. He wasn't thinking about anyone else at all. Now that he'd run out of storage space, God was trying to lead him into the revelation that he had enough to give. He was blessed enough to be a blessing to others.

So He put the question in him: *What shall I do now that I have no more room to store my wealth?*

It was the right question. But, sad to say, the man came up with the wrong answer. He decided to tear down his barns and build bigger ones.

Think about what a foolish decision that was. He was going to have to empty out his old barns before demolishing them. What was he going to do with the crops he'd been storing there? Was he just going to leave them out in the weather while the new barns were being built? They'd be ruined.

Meantime, he was going to spend money like there's no tomorrow, hoping there'd be no crop failure this year. He was not only going into major expenditure mode, he was putting everything at risk. One bad storm, one bad crop year, and he would be destroyed.

It sounds crazy, but that plan seemed right to him.

Why? Because his thinking was clouded by covetousness. He was not looking to God as his source. He had gathered those riches by himself for himself. His purpose in life was to take it easy and have a party. He was making his own way and coming up with his own decisions. Instead of seeking the will of God and listening to Him, the rich man was listening to himself, and he didn't know much.

Covetous thinking had turned him into a fool.

That's not just my assessment—according to Jesus, that's what God called the man. "God said unto him,

Thou fool, this night thy soul shall be required of thee: then whose shall those things be, which thou hast provided?" (verse 20).

Act Like a Wise Man

Here's the sobering end to the story. The man never got a chance to tear down his barns. He never got that far because the decision he made opened the door to death in his life. Covetousness cost him his protection from God and he died that night.

The Bible doesn't say how it happened. Maybe he was murdered. Maybe someone wanted to steal what he had in his barns. Maybe he had a heart attack. We don't know.

But we do know this: *God was trying to get his attention before it happened.* He was prompting the man to ask the right question. But instead of going to God and saying, "Lord, what's the answer to this?" he made up the answer himself. He became his own god.

Whether the economy is good or bad, trying to be your own god is stupid. It makes people think and act like fools.

So don't do it. Act like a wise man instead. Jesus told us how. He said, "Whosoever heareth these sayings of mine, and doeth them, I will liken him unto a wise man" (Matthew 7:24).

Notice, He didn't say we have to be wise on our own. All we have to do is *act* like a wise man to get a wise man's results, and we do that by hearing and obeying God's Word. We do it by following the instructions God gave to Joshua when he was about to lead the Israelites into the Promised Land: "This book of the law shall not depart out of thy mouth; but thou shalt meditate therein day and night, that thou mayest observe to do according to all that is written therein: for then thou shalt make thy way prosperous, and then thou shalt have good success" (Joshua 1:8).

If those instructions worked for Joshua (and they did) they will work for us. He was facing a far more pressurized situation than the one we face today. He was heading into combat, going back to Canaan to fight the giants who had scared the Israelites back into the wilderness 40 years earlier.

You can imagine what the devil was saying to him about it, trying to get him knotted up in fear and worry. He was telling Joshua the giants had gotten bigger since he last saw them. They'd multiplied. They were stronger. *Face it, Joshua. There's no way you and your little ragtag bunch can beat those monsters. You don't know anything about war. They've spent the past 40 years developing their military might while you and your little group of grasshoppers have been wandering around in the desert. Blah...blah...blah...*

But Joshua didn't listen. He kept his attention on God's Word. He believed that if he'd meditate on that Word, think the way it taught him to think, and do what it told him to do, no matter how bad the situation around him became, he'd prosper. He'd have good success and, as one translation puts it, *deal wisely in the affairs of life.*

It's the Same Old System

That's just as true for us today as it was for Joshua. If we'll align our thinking and our actions with The Word, we'll deal wisely in all the affairs of life. We'll succeed. We'll prosper because we're operating according to the wisdom of God.

Don't you think He has this economy figured out? Do you think He's sitting up in heaven wondering how we came up with such a complicated system? Do you think He is saying, "Oh my, I've never seen anything like that!"

No, this is the same old system that's been around since the tower of Babel. It's an economy designed by men trying to meet their own needs without God. It's nothing new.

Even the socialist agenda that

people are so upset about these days made its debut at the tower of Babel. Socialism first reared its head when the builders said, "We'll make this tower out of brick." Unlike the stones with which God builds His temple, bricks are all just alike. God never made any two things alike in all of history. There aren't even two fingerprints alike.

Why is that significant?

It tells us God is interested in the success of the individual. His way is to bring successful individuals together and make them a thousand times more successful together than they were by themselves. That's God's way.

Man's way is to make everyone just alike. Make them all look alike. Don't let anyone get ahead of anyone else. Except, of course, those who are in charge because they're the only ones who know anything and they have to run it all.

That sums up the Babylonian system.

But you and I aren't in that system. We're in the Eden system. We have a covenant with God. We're BLESSED with THE BLESSING of Abraham and God has given us His Word to live by, so no matter what's going on in the world's system we can deal wisely and have good success.

"Brother Copeland, do you really think that's possible in these messed-up financial times?"

I know it is.

That October morning when the Lord spoke to me about the economic disturbance that was coming and the plans people would devise to deal with it, He said if we'd keep listening to Him and doing what He says, if we'd stay completely clean of covetousness, we can live in heaven on earth right in the midst of all the trouble.

Sure enough, that's what's happened. Gloria and I have marveled over it time and again. Right in the middle of all the financial turmoil that's gone on, we've felt almost like we're in heaven. Without any debts and without any cares, we have unhooked from Babylon's system and we're having the time of our lives enjoying THE BLESSING of the kingdom of God.

Prayer for Salvation and Baptism in the Holy Spirit

Heavenly Father, I come to You in the Name of Jesus. Your Word says, "Whosoever shall call on the name of the Lord shall be saved" (Acts 2:21). I am calling on You. I pray and ask Jesus to come into my heart and be Lord over my life according to Romans 10:9–10: "If thou shalt confess with thy mouth the Lord Jesus, and shalt believe in thine heart that God hath raised him from the dead, thou shalt be saved. For with the heart man believeth unto righteousness; and with the mouth confession is made unto salvation." I do that now. I confess that Jesus is Lord, and I believe in my heart that God raised Him from the dead.

I am now reborn! I am a Christian—a child of Almighty God! I am saved! You also said in Your Word, "If ye then, being evil, know how to give good gifts unto your children: HOW MUCH MORE shall your heavenly Father give the Holy Spirit to them that ask him?" (Luke 11:13). I'm also asking You to fill me with the Holy Spirit. Holy Spirit, rise up within me as I praise God. I fully expect to speak with other tongues as You give me the utterance (Acts 2:4). In Jesus' Name. Amen!

Begin to praise God for filling you with the Holy Spirit. Speak those words and syllables you receive—not in your own language, but the language given to you by the Holy Spirit. You have to use your own voice. God will not force you to speak. Don't be concerned with how it sounds. It is a heavenly language!

Continue with the blessing God has given you and pray in the spirit every day.

You are a born-again, Spirit-filled believer. You'll never be the same!

Find a good church that boldly preaches God's Word and obeys it. Become part of a church family who will love and care for you as you love and care for them.

We need to be connected to each other. It increases our strength in God. It's God's plan for us.

Make it a habit to watch the *Believer's Voice of Victory* television broadcast and become a doer of the Word, who is blessed in his doing (James 1:22-25).

About the Author

Kenneth Copeland is co-founder and president of Kenneth Copeland Ministries in Fort Worth, Texas, and best-selling author of books that include *How to Discipline Your Flesh* and *Honor—Walking in Honesty, Truth and Integrity.*

Now in his 43rd year as a minister of the gospel of Christ and teacher of God's Word, Kenneth is the recording artist of such award-winning albums as his Grammy-nominated *Only the Redeemed, In His Presence, He Is Jehovah, Just a Closer Walk* and his most recently released *Big Band Gospel* album. He also co-stars as the character Wichita Slim in the children's adventure videos *The Gunslinger, Covenant Rider* and the movie *The Treasure of Eagle Mountain,* and as Daniel Lyon in the *Commander Kellie and the Superkids*™ videos *Armor of Light* and *Judgment: The Trial of Commander Kellie.*

With the help of offices and staff in the United States, Canada, England, Australia, South Africa and Ukraine, Kenneth is fulfilling his vision to boldly preach the uncompromised Word of God from the top of this world, to the bottom, and all the way around. His ministry reaches millions of people worldwide through daily and Sunday TV broadcasts, magazines, teaching audios and videos, conventions and campaigns, and the World Wide Web.

more help, **more answers**

MORE OF GOD'S PLAN FOR YO

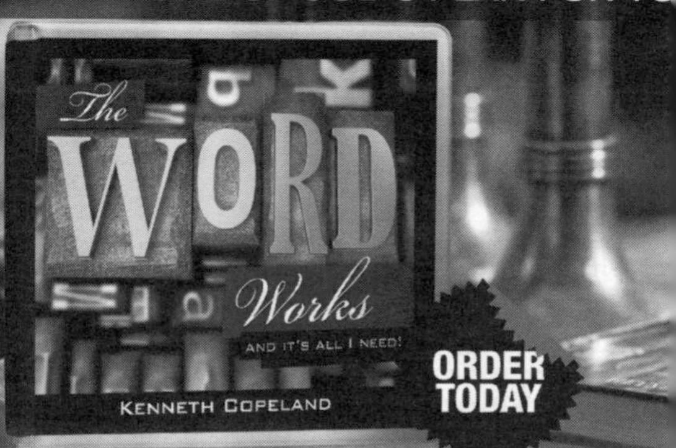

The Word Works (CD) 012450 How do you get the answers you need? In this foundational teaching, Kenneth Copeland shows you how the Word of God is guaranteed to bring results. It carries the ability to produce what you need...every time. In fact, it's all you need.

One Word From God Can Change Your Formula for Success (book) 300714
God created you to win. Learn to make the right decisions on your personal path to success.

God's Success Formula (book) 300532
Stop chasing success. Discover the truth about success in the workplace and in relationships through *God's Success Formula.*

To order these products and view complete catalo
visit us at **kcm.org** or **call 800-600-7395.**

World Offices
Kenneth Copeland Ministries

For more information about KCM and our products, please write to the office nearest you:

Kenneth Copeland Ministries
Fort Worth, TX 76192-0001

Kenneth Copeland
Locked Bag 2600
Mansfield Delivery Centre
QUEENSLAND 4122
AUSTRALIA

Kenneth Copeland
Post Office Box 15
BATH
BA1 3XN
U.K.

Kenneth Copeland
Private Bag X 909
FONTAINEBLEAU
2032
REPUBLIC OF
SOUTH AFRICA

Kenneth Copeland
PO Box 3111 STN LCD 1
Langley BC V3A 4R3
CANADA

Kenneth Copeland Ministries
Post Office Box 84
L'VIV 79000
UKRAINE

We're Here for You!

Join Kenneth and Gloria Copeland and the *Believer's Voice of Victory* broadcasts Monday through Friday and on Sunday each week, and learn how faith in God's Word can take your life from ordinary to extraordinary.

You can catch the *Believer's Voice of Victory* broadcast on your local, cable or satellite channels.* And it's also available 24 hours a day by webcast at BVOV.TV.

Enjoy inspired teaching and encouragement from Kenneth and Gloria Copeland and guest ministers each month in the *Believer's Voice of Victory* magazine. Also included are real-life testimonies of God's miraculous power and divine intervention in the lives of people just like you!

To receive a FREE subscription to
Believer's Voice of Victory, write to:

Kenneth Copeland Ministries
Fort Worth, TX 76192-0001

or call: 800-600-7395
or visit: **kcm.org**

If you are writing from outside the U.S., please contact the KCM office nearest you. Addresses for all Kenneth Copeland Ministries offices are listed on the previous pages.

*Go to kcm.org for times and stations in your area.